Vertical Garden
The Key to Self-Sufficiency in the City

Beginner's Guide to Building
A Self-Suffcient Garden
Even If You Are Short on Growing Space

Modern Green Lifestyle

Modern Green Lifestyle

Modern Green Lifestyle

Table of Contents

Introduction

Vertical gardening is a technique for cultivating plants in a vertical space, typically on a wall, trellis, or other vertical surface, as opposed to in traditional horizontal garden beds. This innovative gardening technique has grown in popularity in recent years, especially in urban areas with limited space. Vertical gardening enables individuals to maximize the use of their space and cultivate a garden in virtually any location, be it a small balcony, courtyard, or rooftop. It is also a great way to add greenery and aesthetic appeal to indoor spaces.

Living walls, green facades, hydroponic systems, pocket gardens, and modular gardens are examples of the various types of vertical gardening systems. Each system has its own distinct features and benefits, allowing for the creation of a vertical garden tailored to an individual's preferences and needs.

Vertical gardening provides numerous benefits in addition to space conservation. It can also help to reduce energy consumption by insulating buildings and decreasing the need for air conditioning, and can be used to cultivate a diverse array of plants, including flowers, herbs, fruits, and vegetables. This can provide fresh produce and the satisfaction of growing one's own food.

The success of a vertical gardening project is contingent on a number of variables, including the chosen system, the plants being grown, and the local environmental conditions.

System selection is one of the most important aspects of a successful vertical garden. Different types of vertical gardening systems have different requirements and limitations, and the success of a garden depends on selecting the appropriate system for the project's particular conditions and objectives. Some systems may be better suited for indoor use, whereas others may be better suited for outdoor environments. When selecting a system, it is essential to consider space, lighting, water availability, and maintenance requirements.

Additionally crucial to the success of a vertical garden is the selection of plants. Not all plants are suitable for vertical gardening, and it is essential to select plants that are well-suited to the garden's specific conditions. Considerations include the amount of available light and water, as well as the garden's climate and environment.

Also essential to the success of a vertical garden is its maintenance. Watering, fertilizing, and pruning the plants regularly are essential for their health and growth. It is also essential to keep an eye out for pests and diseases in the garden and to take immediate action if problems arise.

Vertical gardens are gaining popularity in a variety of settings, including cities, commercial buildings, and private residences. Several factors contribute to this trend.

Vertical gardens: are becoming increasingly popular due in large part to their ability to conserve space. Vertical gardening allows individuals to maximize the use of limited outdoor space in densely populated urban areas by growing plants vertically on walls or other vertical surfaces

- are visually arresting and can add a distinctive and appealing element to any space. They can be designed to produce a variety of effects, including lush green walls and intricate patterns
- can improve air quality and reduce noise pollution, making them an attractive option for urban areas. In addition, they can insulate buildings, which can reduce energy consumption and heating and cooling costs
- having plants around can improve your mood, reduce your stress levels, and even lower your blood pressure. Vertical gardens can provide access to fresh produce, which can contribute to a healthier diet and way of life

- can be used as a branding or marketing tool in commercial settings such as retail stores, restaurants, and hotels, providing a unique and eye-catching element that distinguishes the business from its competitors.

Types of Vertical Gardening Systems

There are several types of vertical gardening systems available, each with its own unique features and benefits.
Each vertical gardening system has its own unique benefits and limitations, and the best system for a particular project will depend on factors such as space, location, climate, and the plants being grown.

Climbing plants are a popular choice for vertical gardening systems, as they can provide a lush and natural green wall that can improve the appearance of any space. Here are some of the most common systems for growing climbing plants:

Trellis systems: Trellises are simple and effective systems that consist of a series of horizontal wires or rods that provide support for climbing plants. They can be used both indoors and outdoors and are easy to install and maintain.

Wall-mounted planters: Wall-mounted planters are containers that are attached to a wall and are used to grow climbing plants. They can be made from a variety of materials, including plastic, metal, and wood, and can be arranged in a variety of configurations to create a custom design.

Vertical wire or mesh systems: Vertical wire or mesh systems are similar to trellises but use a mesh or wire grid to support climbing plants. They can be used both indoors and outdoors and are ideal for creating a natural green wall.

Modular systems: Modular systems consist of a series of interlocking containers that can be stacked to create a vertical garden. They can be used to grow a variety of plants, including climbing plants, and are ideal for areas with limited space.

Green facades: Green facades are similar to living walls but use climbing plants that grow up a wall or trellis rather than being planted in a structure. They are often used to cover unsightly walls or provide shade, and can be particularly effective in urban areas.

Vertical container gardening systems are ideal for small spaces, balconies, and other areas where there is limited space for a traditional garden. Here are some of the most common vertical container gardening systems:

Stacked container gardens: Stacked container gardens are made up of a series of pots that are stacked on top of each other. This system is ideal for growing a variety of plants in a small space.

Hanging container gardens: Hanging container gardens use pots that are suspended from a support structure, such as a wall or ceiling. They are ideal for growing plants in areas with limited floor space.

Pocket planters: Pocket gardens are small, self-contained planters that can be mounted on a wall. They are particularly useful for small spaces, and can be used to grow a variety of plants, including flowers, herbs, and vegetables.

Tower gardens: Tower gardens use a series of stacked containers to grow plants vertically. The containers are arranged in a column, with each container positioned above the one below it. They are ideal for growing a variety of plants, including fruits, vegetables, and herbs.

Modular container gardens: Modular container gardens use interlocking containers that can be arranged in a variety of configurations to create a custom vertical garden. They are ideal for areas with limited space or where soil is not available.

Vertical container gardening systems can be made from a variety of materials, including plastic, metal, and wood. They are ideal for small spaces and can be used to grow a variety of plants, including fruits, vegetables, and herbs. The choice of system will depend on the specific needs of the project, including the space available, the types of plants being grown, and the overall design aesthetic.

When it comes to vertical container gardening, **pocket planters** can be a great option for growing small plants, herbs, and flowers. Pocket planters are small, vertical planters that can be mounted on a wall or fence and are designed with individual pockets or compartments for each plant.

The pockets are typically made of a durable fabric material, such as felt or canvas, that is breathable and allows for good drainage. The plants are inserted into each pocket, and the planter can then be hung on a wall or fence using hooks or a mounting bracket.

Some plants that can work well in pocket planters include herbs like basil, thyme, and parsley, as well as small flowers like petunias and pansies. The pockets can also be used to grow succulents or small vegetables like cherry tomatoes or peppers.

It's important to consider the amount of light, water, and nutrients that each plant will need when choosing what to grow in a pocket planter. Plants that have similar growing requirements should be grouped together in the same pocket or planter to ensure they thrive.

A **vegetable ladder** is a type of vertical gardening system that can be used to grow a variety of vegetables in a small space. Here are some steps to make use of a vegetable ladder:

Choose a location: Select a location that gets plenty of sunlight and has easy access to water. The ladder can be placed against a wall, fence, or other support structure.

Select a ladder: Choose a ladder that is sturdy and has wide rungs that can support the weight of the pots or containers. You can use a wooden ladder or a metal ladder, depending on your preferences.

Add shelves: If your ladder does not already have shelves, you can add them using wood or metal brackets. The shelves should be deep enough to hold your containers or pots.

Choose containers: Select containers that are the right size for the vegetables you want to grow. You can use plastic or terracotta pots, fabric grow bags, or other types of containers. Make sure the containers have drainage holes.

Fill with soil: Fill each container with a good quality potting mix, making sure to leave enough space for the roots of the vegetables.

Plant the vegetables: Plant your chosen vegetables in each container, following the instructions on the seed packets or plant labels. You can grow a variety of vegetables in a vegetable ladder, including tomatoes, cucumbers, lettuce, and herbs.

Water and fertilize: Water your plants regularly, making sure to keep the soil moist but not waterlogged. You can also fertilize your plants with a balanced fertilizer to promote healthy growth.

By using a vegetable ladder, you can make the most of a small space and grow a variety of vegetables in a vertical garden. Just be sure to select the right ladder, containers, and plants, and to provide proper care and maintenance to ensure a successful harvest.

Vertical pots are a type of container used in vertical gardening systems to grow plants vertically, such as on a wall, fence or balcony. Vertical pots are designed to be compact and space-efficient, allowing you to grow more plants in a smaller area. Here are some features of vertical pots:

Design: Vertical pots come in a variety of designs and styles, but they are all designed to be space-efficient and vertically oriented. They can be made from various materials such as plastic, metal, or ceramic.

Mounting: Many vertical pots come with built-in mounting systems that allow them to be easily attached to a wall or other vertical surface. Some pots have hooks or brackets that can be attached to a mounting system, while others are designed to hang from a railing or fence.

Drainage: Good drainage is important for healthy plants, and most vertical pots have drainage holes at the bottom to prevent water from accumulating in the soil. Some pots also have a tray or catch basin at the bottom to collect excess water.

Size and Shape: Vertical pots come in various sizes and shapes to accommodate different types of plants. Some vertical pots are tall and narrow, while others are shorter and wider. The size of the pot should be appropriate for the size of the plant you want to grow.

Planting: You can plant a wide variety of plants in vertical pots, including herbs, flowers, and small vegetables. When planting, make sure to use good quality soil and choose plants that are appropriate for the amount of light and water they will receive in the vertical pot.

Vertical pots can be a great way to add greenery to a small space or to create an eye-catching vertical garden. With the right selection of pots, mounting system, and plants, you can create a beautiful and thriving vertical garden.

A vertical vegetable garden can be a great way to grow fresh produce indoors, even if you don't have a lot of space. Here are some steps to create a vertical vegetable garden indoors:

Choose a location: Select a location in your home that gets plenty of natural light, such as a sunny windowsill or a well-lit corner. If you don't have access to natural light, you can use grow lights to provide artificial light.

Select a vertical gardening system: There are a variety of vertical gardening systems that can be used indoors, such as a hanging garden, a wall-mounted garden, or a freestanding garden. Choose a system that fits your space and your needs.

Choose vegetables: Select vegetables that are suitable for growing indoors, such as leafy greens, herbs, cherry tomatoes, and small peppers. Choose vegetables that don't require a lot of space to grow and that can thrive in the environment you have created.

Choose containers: Select containers that are the right size for the vegetables you want to grow. You can use plastic or terracotta pots, fabric grow bags, or other types of containers. Make sure the containers have drainage holes.

Fill with soil: Fill each container with a good quality potting mix, making sure to leave enough space for the roots of the vegetables.

Plant the vegetables: Plant your chosen vegetables in each container, following the instructions on the seed packets or plant labels. You can plant multiple vegetables in a single container, but make sure not to overcrowd the plants.

Water and fertilize: Water your plants regularly, making sure to keep the soil moist but not waterlogged. You can also fertilize your plants with a balanced fertilizer to promote healthy growth.

Maintain the garden: Regularly check your plants for pests, diseases, and nutrient deficiencies. Prune the plants as necessary to keep them healthy and to prevent overcrowding.

By creating a vertical vegetable garden indoors, you can enjoy fresh produce throughout the year and add a touch of green to your home. Just be sure to select the right vegetables, containers, and care practices to ensure a successful harvest.

In the context of vertical gardening, a frame can refer to a structure that supports the plants in a vertical garden. Frames can be made from a variety of materials, such as wood, metal, or PVC pipe, and can be designed to fit the specific needs of the plants and the space available.

For example, a frame can be used to create a trellis for climbing plants, such as tomatoes, beans, or cucumbers. The frame can be designed to support the weight of the plants and to allow them to climb as they grow. Alternatively, a frame can be used to support a series of hanging baskets or planters, allowing plants to be stacked vertically and maximizing the use of space.

When designing a frame for a vertical garden, it is important to consider the weight and size of the plants, the amount of sunlight they will receive, and the space available for the frame itself. A well-designed frame can help to create a beautiful and functional vertical garden that thrives and produces healthy, fresh produce.

Vertical Gardening Benefits

Vertical gardens are an innovative and space-saving way to grow plants in a smaller area. By utilizing a vertical structure, you can create a lush and green space, even in the smallest of areas. With a vertical garden, you can plant a wide variety of plants, including vegetables, fruits, flowers, and herbs, all in a compact and efficient design.

Vertical gardens can be designed in a variety of ways, including wall-mounted structures, freestanding towers, and hanging planters. They can be customized to fit any space, from small balconies to large commercial buildings. This flexibility allows for a wide range of possibilities when it comes to design and placement.

One of the key benefits of a vertical garden is that it maximizes the use of space. In traditional gardens, plants are typically arranged in rows, with each plant taking up a significant amount of space. In a vertical garden, plants are arranged in tiers, allowing for more plants to be grown in the same area. This not only maximizes space, but also reduces the amount of water and fertilizer needed.

Vertical gardens can also be used to create a unique and visually stunning space. With the right combination of plants and design elements, a vertical garden can be a beautiful and functional addition to any outdoor or indoor space.

Overall, a vertical garden is an innovative and efficient way to grow more plants in a smaller area, while also adding a touch of green to any space.

Vertical gardens allow you to grow plants at a comfortable and accessible height. Unlike traditional gardens where plants are typically grown at ground level, in a vertical garden, plants can be grown at waist level or higher, making them easier to access and care for.

This easy access is particularly beneficial for those with physical limitations or disabilities that make it difficult to bend down or kneel on the ground. With a vertical garden, you can tend to your plants without putting undue strain on your body.

Vertical gardens also make it easier to monitor the health and growth of your plants. Since they are at a comfortable height, you can easily check for pests, disease, or other issues, and take action quickly if needed. This can help you maintain a healthy and thriving garden.

Additionally, vertical gardens can be designed to suit your personal preferences and tastes. You can choose the plants that you want to grow, as well as the design and style of the garden. This allows you to create a garden that is both functional and aesthetically pleasing.

Vertical gardens can offer consistent crop yields year-round by providing a controlled environment for plants. This means that the growing conditions can be optimized for each plant, ensuring they receive the right amount of light, water, and nutrients at all times. Unlike traditional outdoor gardens, where growing conditions can fluctuate due to changes in weather and climate, vertical gardens are shielded from external factors, which means that crop yields can be more consistent over the year.

This controlled environment is achieved through a variety of techniques, such as using LED lights to provide the necessary light spectrum for plant growth and automatic irrigation systems to regulate water levels. By using these methods, it's possible to create the ideal growing conditions for plants, allowing them to grow and produce crops at a consistent rate.

In addition to the controlled environment, vertical gardens can also be designed to maximize the use of space, which can lead to higher crop yields. Since the plants are arranged vertically, they can be placed closer together, allowing for more plants to be grown in the same area. This means that more crops can be produced in the same space, providing higher yields.

Vertical gardens offer the ability to grow a wide variety of plants, which is a significant benefit for gardeners and farmers alike. With a vertical garden, plants are arranged in tiers, allowing for a larger number of plants to be grown in a smaller area. This vertical orientation means that you can grow plants of different types and sizes, from herbs and vegetables to flowers and even small fruit trees.

The customizable design of vertical gardens allows for a range of different plant types to be grown in a small area. Vertical gardens can be designed to fit any space, from small balconies to large commercial buildings, and can be customized to meet your specific needs. Whether you want to grow edible plants, such as herbs and vegetables, or ornamental flowers, a vertical garden can be designed to accommodate your preferences.

Another benefit of vertical gardens is the ability to create a controlled environment for plants. With this type of garden, you can regulate the amount of water, light, and nutrients that each plant receives, ensuring that each plant gets what it needs to thrive. This means that you can grow a wide variety of plants, even those that require specific growing conditions, such as those that need more or less sunlight, water, or soil pH.

Vertical gardens offer an easy-to-maintain gardening option that can be ideal for busy or inexperienced gardeners. The following are some ways that vertical gardens can be low maintenance:

Automatic watering systems: Many vertical garden systems come with automatic watering systems that make it easy to maintain the plants. These systems can be programmed to water the plants on a set schedule, which takes the guesswork out of watering and ensures that the plants get the right amount of water.

Reduced need for weeding: Vertical gardens can be designed to use a soilless growing medium, such as hydroponics or aeroponics, which can reduce the need for weeding. Since the plants are not grown in soil, there are fewer weeds that can grow, which means less maintenance for the gardener.

Vertical orientation: The vertical orientation of the garden makes it easy to access and maintain the plants. This means that you can easily prune, harvest, and maintain the plants without having to bend over or crawl on the ground, making it easier for those with limited mobility.

Reduced pest problems: Vertical gardens can be less prone to pest problems than traditional gardens since the plants are elevated off the ground. This means that pests, such as slugs and snails, have less access to the plants, making it easier to maintain a healthy garden without the need for pesticides.

Vertical gardens offer a significant amount of flexibility when it comes to growth. This is because the design of a vertical garden can be customized to meet the specific needs of the plants being grown, as well as the preferences of the gardener. With a traditional garden, plants must be grown in the ground, limiting their growth potential and the ways in which they can be arranged. A vertical garden, on the other hand, allows for plants to be grown in a vertical orientation, providing more options for growth and arrangement.

One of the key benefits of a vertical garden is the customizable design. Vertical gardens can be created in a wide range of sizes and shapes, and can be tailored to fit the specific needs of the plants being grown. For example, some plants require more space to grow than others, and a vertical garden can be designed to provide this space without taking up too much room. Additionally, different types of plants require different growing conditions, such as different amounts of light, water, and nutrients. A vertical garden can be designed to provide the optimal growing conditions for each plant, allowing for greater flexibility in what can be grown.

Vertical gardens also offer flexibility in terms of the way plants are arranged. Since plants are grown in a vertical orientation, they can be arranged in a variety of ways to create different designs and patterns. This allows for a greater level of creativity and customization, making it possible to create a truly unique and beautiful garden.

One of the key benefits of a vertical garden is that it is easier to protect than a traditional garden. With a vertical garden, the plants are grown in a controlled environment, which makes it easier to protect them from pests, diseases, and harsh weather conditions.

In a traditional garden, plants are exposed to the elements, which can make them vulnerable to pests and diseases. For example, insects such as aphids, snails, and slugs can easily access the plants in a traditional garden and cause damage. Additionally, weather conditions such as heavy rain, strong winds, and extreme temperatures can also cause damage to plants in a traditional garden.

With a vertical garden, however, the plants are grown in a controlled environment, which makes it easier to protect them from pests and weather conditions. For example, a vertical garden can be covered with a protective netting to prevent insects and birds from accessing the plants. Additionally, since the plants are grown in a vertical orientation, they are less likely to be affected by strong winds or heavy rain, which can be more damaging to plants in a horizontal garden.

Furthermore, since a vertical garden can be grown indoors or in a greenhouse, it is possible to completely control the environment in which the plants are grown. This allows for optimal growing conditions and minimizes the risk of pests and diseases.

Water conservation is another significant benefit of vertical gardens. With traditional gardens, plants are typically grown in the ground, which can lead to water waste due to runoff and evaporation. Vertical gardens, on the other hand, allow for a more efficient use of water, which can help to conserve this valuable resource. Here are some of the ways that vertical gardens offer water conservation benefits:

Reduced runoff: Vertical gardens can be designed to capture and retain water, reducing the amount of runoff that occurs. This is especially important in urban areas where runoff can lead to pollution and the loss of soil and nutrients.

Reduced evaporation: Vertical gardens can be designed to provide shade and reduce the amount of sunlight that plants receive, which helps to reduce water evaporation. This means that plants require less water, which can help to conserve this resource.

Efficient irrigation: Vertical gardens can be designed to provide a more efficient irrigation system, ensuring that plants receive the water they need without wasting water. Drip irrigation systems, for example, can be used to provide targeted watering to specific plants, reducing the amount of water that is wasted.

Recycled water: Vertical gardens can be designed to use recycled water, such as rainwater or graywater. This means that less water needs to be drawn from local water sources, helping to conserve this resource.

Vertical gardens offer several benefits when it comes to defending against climate change. One of the primary benefits is the ability to reduce the urban heat island effect. This effect occurs when buildings and paved surfaces absorb and retain heat, causing the temperature in urban areas to rise significantly higher than surrounding rural areas. Vertical gardens can help to mitigate this effect by providing a natural cooling effect, as plants absorb carbon dioxide and other pollutants from the air, releasing oxygen and moisture in return.

Additionally, vertical gardens can help to combat air pollution, which is a significant contributor to climate change. Plants in vertical gardens absorb pollutants from the air, including carbon dioxide, nitrogen oxides, and sulfur dioxide, which can reduce the levels of these harmful gases in the atmosphere. By reducing air pollution, vertical gardens can help to improve air quality, which can have a significant impact on the health and well-being of the people living in the surrounding area.

Vertical gardens can also help to mitigate the effects of climate change by reducing stormwater runoff. In urban areas, stormwater runoff can cause significant damage to infrastructure, including roads and buildings. By capturing and filtering rainwater, vertical gardens can help to reduce the amount of stormwater runoff, protecting the surrounding area from potential flooding and other related issues.

Another significant benefit of vertical gardens is that they are easy to harvest. With a traditional garden, plants are typically grown in the ground, making it difficult to access and harvest fruits, vegetables, and other crops. In contrast, a vertical garden allows for easy access to plants, making it simple to harvest the crops when they are ready. Here are some of the ways that vertical gardens make harvesting easy:

- Accessibility: With a vertical garden, plants are grown in tiers, making it easy to access each plant without having to bend down or crawl on the ground. This means that you can harvest your crops without straining your back or knees, making it a more comfortable and enjoyable experience.
- Organization: Vertical gardens allow for plants to be arranged in a tidy and organized manner, making it easier to keep track of which plants are ready for harvest. This also helps to reduce the risk of accidentally missing a crop that is ready to be picked.
- Protection: Vertical gardens can be designed to provide protection for crops, keeping them safe from pests and other threats. This means that you can be sure that your crops are healthy and ready for harvest when the time comes.

Extimating Costs

The cost of a vertical garden can vary greatly depending on a number of factors, including the size of the garden, the materials used, and the complexity of the design. Here are some general estimates to consider:

Size: The size of your vertical garden will have a big impact on the cost. A small wall planter can cost as little as $20, while a larger installation that covers an entire wall could cost several thousand dollars.

Materials: The materials used to build the vertical garden will also impact the cost. Common materials include wooden pallets, PVC piping, metal frames, and custom-built systems made from materials like stainless steel. The cost of these materials can range from $50 to $500 or more.

Plants: The cost of the plants you choose to use in your vertical garden will also impact the total cost. Some plants are more expensive than others, and you may need to purchase a large number of plants to fill the space. The cost of plants can range from a few dollars per plant to hundreds of dollars for rare or exotic varieties.

Installation: If you are hiring a professional to install your vertical garden, this will also add to the cost. Installation costs can range from a few hundred dollars to several

thousand, depending on the size and complexity of the project.
Labor costs: The cost of labor will depend on the skill level of the workers and the time it takes to complete the project. More experienced workers will charge more per hour than less experienced workers.

Taking all these factors into consideration, the cost of a basic vertical garden can range from a few hundred to several thousand dollars, while a more complex and customized installation could cost tens of thousands of dollars. It's best to consult with a professional landscaper or designer to get a more accurate estimate based on your specific needs and preferences.

The cost of vegetables and fruits will depend on a variety of factors, including the type of produce, the location, and the time of year. In general, fresh produce is more expensive when it is out of season and has to be imported from other regions or countries. On the other hand, buying in-season produce from local farmers markets can be more affordable.
Additionally, the cost of seeds or starter plants for growing your own vegetables and fruits will also vary. Some seeds and plants may be more expensive than others, but investing in high-quality seeds or plants can often lead to a more successful and fruitful harvest.
It is also worth noting that the cost of growing your own produce can be offset by the savings from not having to purchase produce from a store. Additionally, growing your

own produce can provide a sense of satisfaction and a healthier, more sustainable lifestyle.

The cost of flowers for a garden will depend on various factors such as the type of flower, quantity, and the location of purchase. Some factors that affect the cost of flowers are:

Season: The season in which you purchase flowers will impact their cost. Seasonal flowers are generally less expensive as they are more readily available.

Type of flower: The cost of different flowers varies depending on their rarity and the demand for them. Some flowers are more expensive than others because they are harder to grow or require more care.

Quantity: Buying flowers in bulk can help reduce their cost. Purchasing flowers in large quantities can help you get a discount from the supplier.

Location: The cost of flowers may vary depending on the location where they are purchased. Local flower shops may offer flowers at a lower cost than big-box stores.

Cascading plants are a popular choice for vertical gardens as they grow downwards and create a stunning visual display. Some common types of cascading plants for vertical gardens include trailing petunias, ivy, ferns, and succulents.

The cost of cascading plants can vary depending on the specific plant species, the size of the plant, and where you purchase it. Generally, small starter plants will be less expensive than larger, more mature plants. You can find cascading plants at local nurseries, garden centers, or online plant stores.

In addition to the cost of the plants themselves, you may also need to factor in the cost of soil, fertilizers, and other supplies needed to care for your cascading plants.

Overall, the cost of cascading plants for your vertical garden will depend on your specific plant choices and the size of your garden. It is a good idea to do some research and compare prices to find the best deals on the plants you want.

The maintenance and watering cost of a vertical garden will depend on various factors such as the size of the garden, the type of plants used, and the climate of the location. Here are some things to consider when estimating the maintenance and watering costs:

Watering: Since the plants in a vertical garden are arranged vertically, they may require more frequent watering than traditional gardens. The cost of watering the garden will depend on the amount of water used and the cost of water in your area. One way to save on watering costs is to install a drip irrigation system that can be automated and use less water than manually watering the plants.

Fertilizers and soil amendments: The cost of fertilizers and soil amendments will depend on the type of plants you use and their nutrient requirements. It's important to use high-quality fertilizers and soil amendments to ensure the health of your plants.

Pest control: Pest control is essential to keep the plants in your vertical garden healthy. The cost of pest control will depend on the type of pests you encounter and the method of control used.

Pruning and trimming: Pruning and trimming are necessary to maintain the health and appearance of the plants in your vertical garden. The cost of pruning and trimming will depend on the size of the garden and the frequency of maintenance.

Vertical gardens can have both positive and negative economic consequences. Here are some examples:

Positive economic consequences:

Increased property value: A vertical garden can add to the aesthetics and overall value of a property. This can lead to an increase in property value, which can benefit the owner.

Reduced energy costs: A vertical garden can help reduce energy costs by providing shade and insulation. This can be particularly beneficial in urban areas where energy costs are high.

Increased revenue for businesses: Vertical gardens can attract customers to businesses by providing an attractive and unique aesthetic. This can lead to increased revenue and profits for the business.

Increased job opportunities: The installation and maintenance of vertical gardens can create job opportunities for landscapers and gardeners.

Negative economic consequences:

Initial costs: The installation of a vertical garden can be expensive due to the cost of materials and labor. This can be a barrier for some people who may not be able to afford it.

Maintenance costs: The maintenance costs of a vertical garden can also be high, as it requires frequent watering, fertilizing, and pest control. This can add to the overall cost of owning and maintaining a vertical garden.

Limited lifespan: Vertical gardens may have a limited lifespan, as plants may die or need to be replaced over time. This can add to the maintenance costs and reduce the overall value of the garden.

The energy consumption of a vertical garden will depend on several factors, such as the type of lighting used and the level of automation. Here are some examples:

Lighting: If the vertical garden is located indoors, it will require some form of lighting to provide the plants with adequate light. The type of lighting used can impact the energy consumption of the garden. LED grow lights are a popular choice for vertical gardens, as they are energy-efficient and can provide the necessary light spectrum for plant growth.

Irrigation system: An automated irrigation system can help regulate the amount of water used in a vertical garden, reducing the overall energy consumption. The system can be set to water the plants at specific times of the day and can use water-efficient methods such as drip irrigation.

Pumping system: If the vertical garden is located outdoors, a pumping system may be required to move water from a storage tank to the plants. The energy consumption of the pumping system will depend on the type of pump used and the amount of water being moved.

Climate control: In some cases, a vertical garden may require climate control to maintain a consistent temperature and humidity level. This can be achieved through the use of HVAC systems, which can impact the energy consumption of the garden.

Vertical gardens can have a positive impact on pollution levels in urban areas. Here are some ways that vertical gardens can help reduce pollution:

Air purification: Plants are known to absorb pollutants from the air and release oxygen. By having a vertical garden in an urban area, it can help absorb pollutants such as nitrogen dioxide, ozone, and particulate matter, improving air quality in the immediate area.

Reducing the urban heat island effect: Vertical gardens can help reduce the urban heat island effect, which is caused by the excess heat generated by buildings, roads, and other human-made surfaces. By providing shade and evaporative cooling, vertical gardens can help reduce the amount of heat absorbed by buildings and surrounding surfaces, reducing the overall temperature in the area.

Water filtration: Vertical gardens can help filter rainwater and reduce the amount of runoff that enters the sewer system. This can help reduce the amount of pollution that enters the waterways and protect the local ecosystem.

Noise reduction: Vertical gardens can help reduce noise pollution by absorbing sound waves. This can be particularly beneficial in urban areas where noise levels are high.

Start Building Your Vertical Garden – Step-by-Step Process

Having a plan is an important step in building a successful vertical garden. Here are some things to consider when creating a plan for your vertical garden:

Space: Consider the amount of space you have available for your vertical garden. This will help you determine the size and type of vertical gardening system that will work best for your needs.

Light: Determine the amount of natural light your vertical garden will receive. This will help you choose plants that are suitable for the light conditions in your space.

Water: Consider how you will water your vertical garden. This will depend on the type of vertical gardening system you choose and the plants you are growing.

Soil: Choose a good quality potting mix for your vertical garden. The soil should be well-draining and nutrient-rich to support healthy plant growth.

Plants: Choose plants that are suitable for growing in a vertical garden. Consider the space and light requirements of each plant, as well as the amount of water and nutrients it will need to thrive.

Maintenance: Consider the amount of maintenance your vertical garden will require. This will include tasks such as pruning, fertilizing, and pest control.

When selecting a **structure for your vertical garden**, it's important to consider the weight capacity and size of the structure. The structure should be able to support the weight of the plants you will be growing and should fit the space where you plan to install it.

Some popular options for vertical gardening structures include trellises, wall-mounted gardens, hanging gardens, and freestanding gardens. Trellises are ideal for climbing plants, while wall-mounted gardens can be a great option for those with limited space. Hanging gardens are perfect for those who want to create a lush, cascading effect, and freestanding gardens can be a great way to add a vertical element to a larger garden.

It's also important to consider the materials the structure is made from. Wood and metal are popular options for their durability and stability, but you can also find structures made from PVC or other materials.

The key is to choose a structure that fits your needs and the plants you want to grow. Whether you choose a trellis, wall-mounted garden, hanging garden, or freestanding garden, selecting the right structure is an important step in creating a successful and thriving vertical garden.

When **selecting plants for your vertical garden**, you should consider their light requirements, soil requirements, and water needs.

Light requirements: Some plants need full sunlight, while others can thrive in partial shade. Be sure to choose plants that are suitable for the amount of light your vertical garden will receive. If your vertical garden is indoors, you may need to provide supplemental light to help your plants grow.

Soil requirements: Different plants have different soil requirements. Choose plants that are suitable for the type of soil you will be using in your vertical garden. You can use a good quality potting mix or create your own mix using compost and other organic materials.

Water needs: Different plants have different water requirements. Be sure to choose plants that are suitable for the amount of water your vertical garden will receive. Some plants require more water than others, so be sure to choose plants that can tolerate dry conditions if your vertical garden will be in a dry or sunny location.

When choosing plants for your vertical garden, consider plants that are known to do well in vertical gardens, such as herbs, leafy greens, and small flowering plants. These plants are typically compact and do not require a lot of space to grow, making them well-suited for vertical gardens.

It's also important to choose plants that are easy to maintain and care for. Consider plants that are resistant to pests and diseases and do not require a lot of pruning or maintenance.

Ultimately, the key to selecting plants for your vertical garden is to choose plants that are well-suited for the light, soil, and water conditions in your space and that are easy to maintain and care for.

Modern Green Lifestyle

There are many plants that can be grown in a vertical garden, and the specific plants you choose will depend on your personal preferences, the amount of sunlight your space receives, and the growing conditions of your vertical garden. Here are a few examples of plants that are commonly grown in vertical gardens:

- Herbs: Herbs such as basil, thyme, oregano, and mint are well-suited for vertical gardens. They are compact and do not require a lot of space to grow, making them ideal for smaller vertical gardens.
- Leafy greens: Lettuce, kale, spinach, and other leafy greens are great options for vertical gardens. They are easy to grow and require little maintenance, making them an excellent choice for beginners.
- Succulents: Succulents are known for their ability to store water in their leaves, making them well-suited for dry conditions. They come in a variety of shapes and sizes, making them a versatile option for vertical gardens.
- Small flowering plants: Small flowering plants such as pansies, petunias, and marigolds can add a pop of color to your vertical garden. These plants are typically compact and do not require a lot of space to grow.
- Vines: Vines such as morning glory, sweet pea, and climbing roses are ideal for trellises and other vertical structures. They can add height and visual interest to your vertical garden and create a lush, cascading effect.

Designing a vertical garden can be a fun and creative process. Here are some tips to help you get started:

- Determine the size and location of your vertical garden: Before you start designing your vertical garden, you'll need to determine the size and location of your space. Consider the amount of sunlight your space receives, as well as the amount of water and soil you'll need to grow your plants.

- Choose a vertical garden structure: There are many different types of vertical garden structures, including wall-mounted planters, trellises, and hanging baskets. Choose a structure that fits your space and design style.

- Select plants that fit your design aesthetic: When choosing plants for your vertical garden, consider the color, texture, and overall look you want to achieve. You can create a monochromatic design using all one color of plants, or mix and match different colors and textures for a more eclectic look.

- Consider the arrangement of your plants: The arrangement of your plants can have a big impact on the overall look of your vertical garden. Consider arranging your plants in a geometric pattern, or clustering plants together for a more organic look.

- Add accessories and decorative elements: You can add accessories and decorative elements to your vertical garden to enhance the overall design. Consider adding decorative stones, figurines, or other elements to add visual interest to your space.

If you prefer a **formal gardening style**, your vertical garden design should reflect this preference by incorporating structured planters, geometrical shapes, and symmetrical arrangements of plants. A formal design would have a clean, crisp look, with a sense of order and symmetry, and would require careful planning to achieve. The use of geometric shapes and patterns, such as circles, squares, and triangles, would be important, as would the use of clipped hedges or topiaries to add structure to the design.

Informal garden style: This style is more relaxed and natural, and often uses a mix of different plant types and textures. If you prefer an informal garden style, you may want to choose a vertical garden design that uses a mix of different planters, hanging baskets, and other vertical structures to create a layered and textural look. The use of organic shapes and natural materials, such as wood or stone, would be important in achieving an informal look.

Contemporary garden style: This style emphasizes clean lines, minimalism, and the use of modern materials, such as metal, glass, and concrete. If you prefer a contemporary garden style, you may want to choose a vertical garden design that uses sleek, modern planters or hanging structures. The use of bold, simple shapes and monochromatic color schemes would be important, as would the use of modern materials to create a clean, minimalist look.

Cottage garden style: This style is often characterized by an abundance of colorful, cottage-style plants, such as roses, daisies, and lavender. If you prefer a cottage garden style, you may want to choose a vertical garden design that incorporates a mix of colorful, cottage-style plants in a variety of different planters and hanging baskets. The use of natural materials, such as wicker or rattan, would be important in achieving a cozy, cottage-style look.

Scale and proportion are important considerations in vertical garden design, as they can affect the overall visual impact of the garden. Here's how to think about scale and proportion when designing your vertical garden:

Scale: Scale refers to the relative size of objects in the garden. A vertical garden that is too large or too small in relation to its surroundings can look out of place or unbalanced. Consider the size of the space you have available for your vertical garden, as well as the size of the plants and other features you want to include in your design. You'll want to choose a scale that complements the surrounding architecture and landscape, rather than competing with it.

Proportion: Proportion refers to the relationship between different elements in the garden. The right proportion can create a sense of harmony and balance, while the wrong proportion can make a garden feel disjointed or overwhelming. Consider the size and shape of your planters and other vertical structures, and make sure they are in proportion to the size of the plants and other elements you plan to include in your design. You may also want to consider the proportions of the surrounding landscape and architecture when choosing your vertical garden design.

Whether **your vertical garden is permanent or temporary** can have an impact on your design considerations. Here's how to think about this factor:

Permanent vertical garden: If your vertical garden is permanent, you'll want to think carefully about the materials you use and the installation process. Consider using high-quality, durable materials that can withstand the elements over time. You may also want to work with a professional installer to ensure that your vertical garden is securely and safely attached to your building or structure.

Temporary vertical garden: If your vertical garden is temporary, you may be able to use more lightweight or portable materials, such as fabric planters or modular systems. You'll also want to think about the installation process and make sure that your vertical garden is easy to install and remove. Portable or modular systems can be a good choice if you're looking for a temporary vertical garden that you can move or change as needed.

In either case, it's important to consider the lifespan of your vertical garden and plan accordingly. If you're creating a permanent garden, you may want to choose plants that will thrive in the space over the long term. If you're creating a temporary garden, you may want to choose plants that are easy to replace or move as needed.

When planning the **height of your vertical garden**, you should start by considering the available space where you'll be installing it. You'll want to measure the wall or structure and take note of any obstacles that may limit the height of your garden, such as windows, vents, or other architectural features. It's important to make sure that your garden won't interfere with any of these elements or create any safety hazards.

Once you have a good sense of the available space, you can start thinking about the overall height of your garden. If you have a large space to work with, you may want to consider a taller garden that can make a bold visual impact. However, if your space is more limited, a shorter garden may be more practical and easier to maintain.

You should also consider the types of plants you'll be using in your vertical garden, as this can impact the height of your design. Some plants, such as trailing vines or creeping groundcovers, may work well in a shorter garden where they can spill over the edges and create a lush, cascading effect. Other plants, such as tall grasses or flowering shrubs, may require a taller garden to accommodate their height and growth habit.

Finally, you should think about the practical considerations of maintaining your vertical garden at its intended height. You'll need to make sure that you can easily access all areas of the garden for watering, pruning, and other maintenance tasks, so consider the height of your garden in relation to your own height and reach. You may also want to consider installing irrigation systems or other features to make maintenance easier and more efficient.

When planning your vertical garden, it's important to **consider the strength and weight-bearing capacity of the structure** that will support it. This is especially important if you're installing your garden indoors or on a wall that wasn't specifically designed for a garden.

If you're installing your garden on an existing wall or structure, you'll need to make sure that it can support the weight of the garden and the plants, as well as any soil or other growing medium that you'll be using. This may require consulting with a structural engineer or other professional to ensure that your design is safe and won't cause any damage to the building.

You'll also need to consider the strength and durability of the materials you'll be using to build your vertical garden. For example, you'll want to choose sturdy, weather-resistant materials that can withstand the elements and won't deteriorate over time. This may include materials like metal or high-grade plastics, as well as durable fabrics or other materials that can withstand exposure to moisture, sunlight, and other environmental factors.

In addition to considering the strength and weight of your structure, you should also think about the weight of your plants and growing medium. Some plants and soil mixes can be quite heavy, so it's important to choose plants that are appropriate for the structure you'll be using and the weight-bearing capacity of your support system. You may also want to consider using lightweight, porous growing media like coconut coir or perlite, which can help reduce the overall weight of your garden while still providing adequate moisture and nutrients for your plants.

By taking the time to consider the strength and weight of your vertical garden, you can ensure that your design is safe, durable, and capable of supporting your plants and your vision for your space.

When planning a vertical garden, it's also important to consider **harvesting flexibility**. Depending on the type of plants you choose and the structure of your garden, harvesting may require some extra effort, so it's helpful to think about how you can make the process as easy as possible.

One consideration is the accessibility of your plants. If your garden is installed high up on a wall, it may be difficult to reach the plants for pruning or harvesting. To make things easier, you may want to consider incorporating a ladder or other safe means of accessing your plants. Alternatively, you could plan your garden so that the plants that require the most attention are installed at a more accessible height.

Another consideration is the type of plants you choose to grow. Some plants, such as herbs and lettuces, are ideal for vertical gardens because they can be harvested as needed, without requiring you to uproot the entire plant. Other plants, like tomatoes or peppers, may require more intensive harvesting, such as picking the fruits when they are ripe. To make things easier, you could plan your garden so that these plants are located at a more accessible height or at the front of your structure.

Ultimately, the key to harvesting flexibility is to plan ahead and think about the types of plants you'll be growing and the ways in which you'll need to access them. With a bit of creativity and ingenuity, you can create a vertical garden that not only looks beautiful but is also easy to maintain and harvest.

If you're interested in creating a vertical garden, one of the first steps is to **select a wall** that will serve as the backdrop for your plants. When selecting a wall, there are a few key things to keep in mind.

First, consider the amount of sunlight that the wall receives. Most plants require at least 6-8 hours of direct sunlight each day, so it's important to choose a wall that gets adequate sunlight. If the wall is in a shaded area, you may need to install supplemental lighting to ensure that your plants thrive.

Next, think about the size of the wall and the amount of space you have to work with. A larger wall will give you more space to plant, but may also be more difficult to maintain. If you're just starting out with vertical gardening, it may be best to choose a smaller wall to begin with.

Once you've selected your wall, you'll need to prepare it for planting. This may involve cleaning the wall and patching any holes or cracks, as well as installing a support structure to hold your plants in place. Depending on the type of structure you choose, you may need to install brackets, hooks, or wires to support your plants.

From there, you can begin planting your vertical garden. You may choose to use a variety of plants, such as flowers, herbs, and vegetables, depending on your preferences and the amount of sunlight your wall receives. Be sure to follow planting instructions carefully, and water and fertilize your plants as needed to ensure they thrive. Over time, your vertical garden will grow and flourish, providing a beautiful and unique backdrop for your outdoor space.

Once you have selected the wall and prepared it for planting, the next step in creating a vertical garden is to **create a framework for your plants**. This framework will serve as the support structure for your plants, helping them to grow and thrive in a vertical orientation.

There are many different types of frameworks that can be used for vertical gardening, depending on your preferences and the specific plants you plan to use. Some popular options include trellises, wire mesh, or hanging baskets.

When creating your framework, be sure to consider the weight and size of your plants. You will want to choose a sturdy framework that can support the weight of your plants as they grow, and that is sized appropriately to allow for ample growth.

Once your framework is in place, you can begin planting your vertical garden. Be sure to follow the specific planting instructions for each type of plant you use, and be sure to water and fertilize your plants as needed to encourage healthy growth.

As your plants begin to grow and thrive, you may need to periodically adjust your framework to accommodate their growth. This could involve adding additional support, or adjusting the size or placement of your existing framework.

With proper care and maintenance, a vertical garden can be a beautiful and unique addition to any outdoor space, allowing you to grow a wide variety of plants in a limited amount of space.

After creating the framework for your vertical garden, the next step is to **set up a water system** to ensure your plants receive the necessary hydration.

The type of water system you use will depend on the size and complexity of your vertical garden, as well as your personal preferences. Some options to consider include:

Drip Irrigation: This system involves placing small tubes or emitters throughout your vertical garden that slowly release water directly to the roots of your plants. This is an efficient system that minimizes water waste.

Hand Watering: If you have a small vertical garden, you may prefer to simply water your plants by hand with a watering can or hose.

Recirculating System: This is a closed system that recirculates water through your garden, minimizing water waste and reducing the need for frequent watering.

No matter which water system you choose, be sure to water your plants regularly to keep them healthy and thriving. The frequency and amount of water needed will depend on the specific plants in your vertical garden, as well as the climate and environment in which they are growing. You may need to experiment with different watering schedules and techniques to find the optimal balance for your garden.

Once you have selected and installed your water system, the next step in the process of vertical gardening is to **connect the irrigation system to a water source and add a fertilizer injector** to ensure your plants receive the necessary nutrients.

To connect the irrigation system to the water source, you will need to run a water line from your home or an outdoor spigot to your vertical garden. This line can be buried underground or run along the surface, depending on your specific situation.

Once you have the water line in place, you can connect it to your irrigation system and add a fertilizer injector to help provide the necessary nutrients to your plants. A fertilizer injector is a device that adds liquid fertilizer to the water as it flows through the irrigation system, ensuring your plants receive a consistent supply of nutrients.

When selecting a fertilizer injector, consider the type of fertilizer you plan to use, as well as the size and complexity of your vertical garden. Some injectors are designed for small-scale systems, while others are better suited for larger or more complex setups.

It is important to follow the manufacturer's instructions carefully when installing and using a fertilizer injector, as improper use can lead to over-fertilization or damage to your plants. With proper care and attention, however, a fertilizer injector can be an effective way to help your plants thrive in a vertical garden.

After you have created the framework and set up the irrigation system with a fertilizer injector, the next step in the process of vertical gardening is to **insert your plants into the pockets or containers.**

Before inserting the plants, make sure that the soil mix is appropriate for the type of plants you have selected. It should be loose and well-draining, but also retain moisture and nutrients.

When inserting the plants, gently loosen the root ball and remove any dead or damaged foliage. Then, carefully insert the plant into the pocket or container, making sure that it is planted at the correct depth and that the soil is firmed around the roots.

Depending on the size of the plant, you may need to add additional soil to the container or pocket to ensure that it is properly supported. You can also use supports like trellises or stakes to help your plants grow upward, depending on the type of plant you are growing.

Once you have inserted all of your plants, make sure to water them thoroughly and check the irrigation system to ensure that it is functioning properly. As your plants grow, you may need to adjust the irrigation system or provide additional support to help them thrive in their vertical environment.

Indoor and Outdoor Vertical Gardening

Indoor vertical gardening and outdoor vertical gardening have some notable differences. One major difference is that indoor plants require artificial lighting, as they do not receive enough sunlight, while outdoor plants grow under direct sunlight. This means that indoor gardeners need to install appropriate lighting systems, which can be quite expensive.

Another difference is in temperature control. Indoor vertical gardens have a stable environment with controlled temperatures, while outdoor plants are exposed to varying temperatures throughout the day and from season to season. As a result, indoor plants can grow year-round, while outdoor plants may need to be harvested before winter sets in.

Watering is another area where indoor and outdoor vertical gardening differ. Outdoor plants receive rainwater, while indoor plants need to be watered manually. The frequency of watering depends on the plant and its location, as well as the type of growing medium used.

Humidity is also an important consideration for indoor vertical gardening. Plants require a certain level of humidity to thrive, which may require the use of a humidifier or regular spraying of water around the plants. Soil is another factor that differs between indoor and outdoor vertical gardening. While outdoor plants grow in natural soil, indoor plants require a growing medium such as peat moss or coco coir.

Pests and diseases are also more of a concern in indoor vertical gardening, as the controlled environment may create a favorable breeding ground for certain pests and diseases. However, indoor plants are less exposed to outdoor elements such as wind and rain, which can help to reduce pest and disease problems.

Finally, indoor vertical gardens are typically smaller than outdoor gardens due to space constraints, which limits the number and types of plants that can be grown indoors. Overall, the key difference between indoor and outdoor vertical gardening is the level of control over the environment in which the plants grow. Outdoor gardening is subject to natural weather patterns, while indoor gardening provides a more controlled environment with artificial lighting, temperature, and humidity.

The process of **indoor vertical gardening** is similar to outdoor vertical gardening, but with some modifications to account for the indoor environment. Here are the steps to get started with indoor vertical gardening:

Choose your plants: Select plants that are suitable for indoor growing conditions and that will thrive in a vertical garden. Consider factors such as light requirements, temperature, and humidity.

Choose your location: Identify a suitable wall or space in your home that will accommodate your vertical garden. Consider factors such as access to natural light, proximity to a water source, and the weight that the structure can support.

Create a framework: Use a freestanding structure or wall-mounted system to create the framework for your vertical garden. Make sure that the structure is securely anchored to the wall or floor.

Set up an irrigation system: Install an irrigation system to deliver water and nutrients to your plants. Depending on the size and complexity of your vertical garden, you may want to consider using a drip irrigation system, a sub-irrigation system, or a hand-watering system.

Install grow lights: If your indoor space does not receive sufficient natural light, you may need to install grow lights to provide the right spectrum and intensity of light for your plants.

Insert plants: Once you have created the framework and set up the irrigation system and grow lights, it's time to insert your plants. Follow the same steps as for outdoor vertical gardening, making sure that the soil mix is appropriate for indoor growing conditions.

Monitor and maintain: Regularly monitor your plants for signs of stress or disease, and make adjustments to the irrigation system or grow lights as needed. Water your plants as necessary, and provide additional support as they grow.

When planning your **outdoor vertical garden,** consider the size of the area, the amount of sunlight the area receives, and the climate. Think about the types of plants you want to grow and how many plants you want to include in your garden. You can also consider adding features such as trellises, arbors, or other structures to support your plants.

To start your outdoor vertical garden, you will first need to select a suitable location with plenty of sunlight and good drainage. Once you have identified the area, you can start planning your vertical garden.

Consider the size of the area and the amount of sunlight it receives, as well as the climate of your region. Think about the types of plants you want to grow and how many you want to include in your garden. You can also consider adding features such as trellises or other structures to support your plants.

Before you can start planting, you will need to prepare the wall or structure that you will be using for your vertical garden. Make sure it is clean and sturdy enough to support the weight of the plants and any supporting structures.

Next, you can install the support system for your plants. This can include trellises, wires, or other structures that will hold the plants in place. Make sure your support system is securely attached to the wall or structure.

Once your support system is in place, you can install the irrigation system. This can include a drip system or other type of irrigation that will deliver water and nutrients to your plants.

Finally, you can start planting your chosen plants in the designated areas on the support system. Make sure to choose plants that are appropriate for the amount of sunlight and water they will receive in your outdoor vertical garden. With proper care and maintenance, your outdoor vertical garden can flourish and provide a beautiful and unique addition to your outdoor space.

Vertical Garden Techniques

Trellising is a technique commonly used in vertical gardening, especially for climbing plants, to help them grow upward and maintain their form. Trellising involves the use of a sturdy framework, such as a lattice or wire mesh, that is placed against a wall or structure to support the plant. As the plant grows, it is trained to climb up the framework, with the use of ties or clips to hold it in place.

The advantage of trellising is that it allows for efficient use of space and provides the necessary support for climbing plants, preventing them from sprawling and taking up too much ground space. Trellising can also help to keep plants off the ground, reducing the risk of pests and diseases, and allowing for better air circulation and sunlight exposure.

Trellising can be done using a variety of materials, such as bamboo, wood, metal or plastic, depending on the size and weight of the plants being grown, as well as the design aesthetic of the gardener. It is important to ensure that the trellis is securely anchored to the wall or structure, to prevent it from toppling over or damaging the plants.

To make a trellis for your garden, you will need the following materials:

- Wooden stakes or poles

- String or twine
- Scissors or a cutting tool
- Hammer
- Nails or screws

Here are the steps to create a trellis for your garden using a teepee-style design:

Choose the location for your trellis. Find an area where your plants will receive adequate sunlight and where the trellis will be stable.

Determine the height and width of your trellis. Consider the size of the plants you will be growing and plan accordingly.

Cut several wooden stakes or poles to the desired height of your trellis. You'll want to have at least three poles for a teepee-style trellis.

Bundle the poles together and tie them together at the top with string or twine.

Spread the poles out to form a tripod shape, then hammer them into the ground to anchor them in place.

Use more string or twine to tie the poles together at intervals to create a grid pattern. This will provide more stability for the plants as they grow up the trellis.

Finally, train your plants to grow up the trellis by tying them to the strings or twine using plant ties. As the plants grow, you can continue to tie them to the trellis to help support their weight.

A **teepee trellis** is a type of trellis that is easy to construct and ideal for supporting climbing plants. To make a teepee trellis, you will need the following materials:

Four to six bamboo or wooden poles, about 6-8 feet long
Garden twine or string
Here's how to make a teepee trellis:

- First, select a location for your teepee trellis. It should be in a sunny spot and have plenty of room for your climbing plants to grow.
- Gather your bamboo or wooden poles and tie them together at the top using garden twine or string. Make sure they are tied tightly so that the structure will be stable.
- Spread the poles out so that they form a cone shape. The bottom of the poles should be about 1-2 feet apart.
- Push the bottom of each pole into the ground, making sure they are secure. You may need to dig small holes for the poles if the ground is hard.
- Once the poles are securely in the ground, use garden twine or string to tie each pole to the one next to it, about halfway up. This will create the structure of the teepee trellis.
- You can now plant your climbing plants at the base of the teepee trellis. As they grow, you can guide them up the poles using garden twine or string.
- A teepee trellis is a simple and effective way to support climbing plants such as beans, peas, and morning glories. It can also add an interesting vertical element to your garden.

A **vertical plant wall** is a popular technique used in vertical gardening that involves attaching a variety of plants to a wall to create a living wall. The wall can be either indoors or outdoors, and the plants can be arranged in a pattern or design to create a visual display.

To create a vertical plant wall, you will need to start by selecting a wall that has adequate exposure to light and is suitable for mounting a vertical garden. Then, you will need to choose the plants that you want to use, based on their lighting and watering requirements.

Next, you will need to install a support structure for the plants. This can be a specialized system designed for vertical gardening, or you can create your own by attaching planters or containers to the wall.

Once the support structure is in place, you can begin planting your chosen plants. Make sure to plant them in a way that allows for adequate growth and airflow, as well as easy maintenance and watering.

To keep your vertical plant wall healthy and thriving, you will need to regularly prune and water the plants, as well as monitor their growth to ensure that they are not overcrowding each other. With proper care, a vertical plant wall can provide a beautiful and sustainable addition to your home or garden.

Caging is a technique used in vertical gardening that involves using a wire or mesh cage to support plants as they grow upward. The cage can be made from various materials, such as bamboo, wood, or metal, and can be placed around individual plants or used to enclose an entire vertical garden.

The cage provides a sturdy structure for plants to climb and helps to prevent them from toppling over or becoming damaged in heavy wind or rain. Cages can be customized to fit the specific needs of the plants being grown, with larger cages used for plants that grow tall and bushy and smaller cages used for plants that are more compact.

Caging can be a simple and effective way to support vertical gardens, especially for plants that have a tendency to sprawl or become too heavy for other support structures. The cages can be reused year after year and can be easily moved or adjusted as needed.

Staking is a common vertical gardening technique used to support tall or climbing plants. It involves the use of stakes or poles that are driven into the ground near the plant and tied to the stem or branches of the plant to provide support.

To stake a plant, you will need to choose a sturdy stake that is taller than the plant you want to support. Drive the stake firmly into the ground, a few inches away from the plant, at a depth that will provide adequate support. Tie the stem or branches of the plant to the stake using a soft, flexible material such as twine or plant ties. Make sure that the ties are not too tight and that they do not damage the plant. As the plant grows, you may need to adjust the ties to provide additional support.

Staking is a simple and effective way to support tall or climbing plants and prevent them from toppling over. It is commonly used for plants like tomatoes, peppers, and beans, but can be used for a wide range of plants that need extra support.

"Training" is a technique used in vertical gardening to direct the growth of plants in a particular direction. This can be accomplished by gently bending the stems or branches of the plant and attaching them to the desired position on a support, such as a trellis or stake. Vining plants, such as tomatoes and cucumbers, are frequently trained to grow upward instead of sprawling on the ground. In order to maximize space and light in a vertical garden, the process of training requires regular monitoring and adjustments as the plant grows.

Vertical containers are specially designed pots or containers that allow plants to grow in a vertical orientation, either by hanging them on a wall or suspending them from a frame. These containers can be made of a variety of materials such as plastic, metal, or ceramic, and come in a range of shapes and sizes.

The advantage of using vertical containers is that they maximize growing space, making them ideal for those with limited gardening space. In addition, they are portable and can be easily moved around, allowing you to change the look of your garden from time to time.

When using vertical containers, it is important to choose plants that are suitable for this type of gardening. You can use a variety of plants, such as flowers, herbs, and vegetables, as long as they have a shallow root system and can grow well in limited soil. To maintain healthy plants in vertical containers, it is also important to regularly water and fertilize them, and to provide adequate light and ventilation.

Vertical herb gardens are a great way to grow herbs when you have limited space or want to add some greenery to your indoor or outdoor living space. Here are some herbs that are well-suited for growing vertically:

Basil: Basil is a popular herb that is easy to grow and maintain. It can be grown in small pots, window boxes, or hanging baskets.

Thyme: Thyme is a hardy herb that grows well in a vertical garden. It can be grown in pots, planters, or in between stones or bricks.

Oregano: Oregano is another herb that can be grown vertically. It thrives in well-draining soil and needs plenty of sunlight.

Parsley: Parsley is a versatile herb that can be used in many different dishes. It grows well in vertical gardens and can be grown in small pots or containers.

Mint: Mint is a great herb for vertical gardens because it spreads quickly and can grow in a variety of environments, including pots and hanging baskets.

Rosemary: Rosemary is a woody herb that grows well in vertical gardens. It prefers well-draining soil and plenty of sunlight.

Sage: Sage is a popular herb that is often used in stuffing, meats, and other dishes. It can be grown in small pots or containers and needs well-draining soil.

When growing herbs vertically, it's important to choose the right type of container and soil. The container should have good drainage and the soil should be well-draining to prevent the roots from becoming waterlogged. Additionally, herbs grown in vertical gardens will need more frequent watering than those grown in traditional gardens, as they tend to dry out more quickly.

Planters affixed to a wall or a shelving system can be a great way to add some greenery to your indoor or outdoor living space. Here are some tips for using planters in this way:

- Choose the right type of planter: When choosing a planter to affix to a wall or shelving system, it's important to select one that is designed for this purpose. Look for planters that are lightweight and have a flat back, so they can be easily mounted onto a wall or shelving system.

- Consider the weight: Make sure to consider the weight of the planter when affixing it to a wall or shelving system. You may need to use anchors or special hardware to ensure that the planter stays securely in place.

- Choose the right plants: Not all plants are well-suited for growing in a planter affixed to a wall or shelving system. Look for plants that are lightweight and don't require a lot of soil, such as succulents, ferns, or trailing vines.

- Use the right soil: When planting in a planter affixed to a wall or shelving system, it's important to use the right type of soil. Look for lightweight potting mixes that are designed for use in containers.

- Consider the lighting: Plants that are affixed to a wall or shelving system may not receive as much natural light as those grown in traditional planters. Make sure to choose plants that can thrive in low-light environments or consider using artificial lighting to supplement the natural light.
- Water regularly: Plants grown in planters affixed to a wall or shelving system may require more frequent watering than those grown in traditional planters. Make sure to water your plants regularly and check the soil to ensure that it stays moist but not waterlogged.

Plant pockets in a retaining wall are a great way to add some greenery to a vertical space while also helping to prevent soil erosion. Here are some tips for creating plant pockets in a retaining wall:

Choose the right plants: When choosing plants for your plant pockets, look for varieties that are well-suited for growing in small spaces and don't require a lot of soil. Succulents, trailing vines, and ferns are all good options.

Choose the right location: Make sure to choose a location for your plant pockets that receives enough sunlight for the plants you've chosen. You'll also want to consider the drainage of the area and make sure that water doesn't pool in the plant pockets.

Prepare the plant pockets: To create a plant pocket, cut a hole in the retaining wall where you want to place the plant. The hole should be slightly larger than the size of the plant container. You can use a saw or drill to cut the hole, being careful not to damage the structure of the retaining wall.

Add soil: Once you've created the plant pocket, add some soil to the bottom. Make sure to use a lightweight, well-draining soil mix that is appropriate for the plants you've chosen.

Insert the plant: Carefully insert the plant container into the plant pocket, making sure that it's firmly in place. Add more soil around the sides of the container, filling in any gaps.

Water regularly: Plants in plant pockets may require more frequent watering than those grown in traditional planters. Make sure to water your plants regularly and check the soil to ensure that it stays moist but not waterlogged.

A pallet garden is a creative and sustainable way to grow plants and vegetables in a small space, and is also an upcycling project since it reuses old pallets. Here are some steps to create a pallet garden:

Choose the right pallet: Make sure to choose a pallet that is in good condition, without any broken or rotting pieces. Also, look for pallets that have been heat-treated instead of chemically treated, as this will ensure that they are safe for growing plants.

Clean the pallet: Clean the pallet thoroughly, removing any dirt or debris that might be stuck in the crevices.

Prepare the pallet: Sand the pallet to smooth out any rough edges or splinters, and apply a coat of paint or sealant if desired.

Add landscape fabric: Add a layer of landscape fabric to the bottom of the pallet, stapling it in place.

Add soil: Fill each of the openings in the pallet with soil. Make sure to use a lightweight, well-draining soil mix that is appropriate for the plants you've chosen.

Plant your garden: Once the soil is in place, you can plant your garden. Choose plants that are well-suited for growing in small spaces and don't require a lot of soil. Herbs, strawberries, lettuce, and small vegetables like radishes or cherry tomatoes are good options.

Water regularly: Make sure to water your plants regularly and check the soil to ensure that it stays moist but not waterlogged.

Making a planter out of a pallet is a creative and sustainable way to add some greenery to your living space. Here are some steps to create a pallet planter:

Choose the right pallet: Make sure to choose a pallet that is in good condition, without any broken or rotting pieces. Also, look for pallets that have been heat-treated instead of chemically treated, as this will ensure that they are safe for growing plants.

Clean the pallet: Clean the pallet thoroughly, removing any dirt or debris that might be stuck in the crevices.

Disassemble the pallet: Use a saw to carefully cut the pallet apart. Remove the slats that make up the top and bottom of the pallet, leaving the middle section intact.

Build the planter: Use the slats that you removed from the pallet to build the sides of the planter. Cut the slats to the desired length and nail or screw them to the middle section of the pallet to create a box.

Add a bottom: To prevent soil from falling out of the bottom of the planter, add a piece of landscape fabric or chicken wire to the bottom of the box.

Add soil: Fill the planter with soil. Make sure to use a lightweight, well-draining soil mix that is appropriate for the plants you've chosen.

Plant your garden: Once the soil is in place, you can plant your garden. Choose plants that are well-suited for growing in small spaces and don't require a lot of soil. Herbs, strawberries, lettuce, and small vegetables like radishes or cherry tomatoes are good options.

Water regularly: Make sure to water your plants regularly and check the soil to ensure that it stays moist but not waterlogged.

Making a garden out of leaning pallets is a creative way to create a vertical garden that can maximize your growing space. Here are some steps to create a garden out of leaning pallets:

Choose the right pallets: Make sure to choose pallets that are in good condition, without any broken or rotting pieces. Also, look for pallets that have been heat-treated instead of chemically treated, as this will ensure that they are safe for growing plants.

Clean the pallets: Clean the pallets thoroughly, removing any dirt or debris that might be stuck in the crevices.

Lean the pallets against a wall or fence: Arrange the pallets in a way that they lean against a wall or fence. Make sure to space them out evenly and at a slight angle to prevent soil from falling out.

Add landscape fabric: Add a layer of landscape fabric to the back and bottom of each pallet, stapling it in place.

Add soil: Fill each of the openings in the pallets with soil. Make sure to use a lightweight, well-draining soil mix that is appropriate for the plants you've chosen.

Plant your garden: Once the soil is in place, you can plant your garden. Choose plants that are well-suited for growing in small spaces and don't require a lot of soil. Herbs, strawberries, lettuce, and small vegetables like radishes or cherry tomatoes are good options.

Water regularly: Make sure to water your plants regularly and check the soil to ensure that it stays moist but not waterlogged.

Maintenance

Water Maintenance
Maintaining a vertical garden's water needs is crucial for ensuring the health and growth of your plants. Here are some tips for maintaining proper water levels in your vertical garden:
Install a water irrigation system: Installing a drip irrigation system can help to keep your plants hydrated and healthy. This system can be set on a timer, ensuring that your plants receive the appropriate amount of water at regular intervals.
Use a moisture meter: A moisture meter can help you determine when your plants need watering. These devices measure the moisture content of the soil, and can be a helpful tool in ensuring that your plants receive the appropriate amount of water.
Choose the right plants: Choose plants that are well-suited for a vertical garden and require less water. Succulents, ferns, and herbs are good options, as they do not need as much water as other plants.
Mulch: Mulching your plants can help to conserve moisture in the soil. Mulch can help prevent evaporation, keeping the soil moist for longer.

Monitor weather conditions: Monitor the weather conditions and adjust your watering schedule accordingly. In hot, dry weather, your plants will require more water than during cooler, wetter weather.

Check for drainage: Ensure that your vertical garden has adequate drainage. Overwatering can be just as harmful to plants as underwatering, and can cause root rot and other problems.

Weed Control

Vertical gardens are a great way to add greenery to small spaces or to enhance the aesthetics of a building. However, with any type of gardening, weed control is an essential task that cannot be ignored. The presence of weeds in a vertical garden can reduce the overall appearance of the garden and may even compete with the plants for nutrients and space.

The first step in weed control is prevention. This means ensuring that the soil in the vertical garden is free of weed seeds and that the garden is planted in a weed-free area. Using a weed barrier cloth or a layer of mulch can also help to prevent weeds from growing.

The second method is hand weeding. Regularly inspect your vertical garden and pull out any weeds that you find by hand. This method is best suited for small gardens that have only a few weeds.

Another effective method for weed control in a vertical garden is the use of natural weed killers. Vinegar, salt, and baking soda are some examples of natural weed killers that can be used in moderation to control weeds in your vertical garden. Be careful not to overuse these products, as they can also harm desirable plants.

Selective herbicides can also be used to control weeds in a vertical garden. These products work by killing only the weeds and not the desirable plants. However, it is important to use herbicides carefully, as some can be harmful to the environment and may harm desirable plants if not used properly.

Fertilization

Fertilizing a vertical garden is a crucial aspect of maintaining healthy and vibrant plants. Without proper nutrients, plants in a vertical garden can struggle to grow and may not reach their full potential. Fertilizer contains the essential nutrients that plants need to grow, such as nitrogen, phosphorus, and potassium.

The first step in fertilizing a vertical garden is to choose the right fertilizer. There are many different types of fertilizers available, including organic and synthetic options. Organic fertilizers are made from natural materials, such as compost or manure, and are a great choice for those who prefer a more natural approach. Synthetic fertilizers, on the other hand, are made from chemicals and are often more concentrated, providing a quick boost of nutrients to the plants.

Once you have chosen the right fertilizer, the next step is to apply it properly. The amount and frequency of fertilizer application depend on the type of plants in your vertical garden, the size of the garden, and the type of fertilizer you are using. It is important to follow the instructions on the fertilizer package carefully, as applying too much fertilizer can damage or even kill your plants.

Another essential aspect of fertilization is to ensure that the fertilizer is distributed evenly throughout the vertical garden. This can be challenging in a vertical garden, as water tends to flow downwards, carrying the fertilizer with it. To overcome this, you can apply the fertilizer in small amounts and water the plants slowly to allow the fertilizer to be absorbed by the plants.

Finally, it is important to note that not all plants in a vertical garden require the same amount or type of fertilizer. Some plants, such as herbs, require less fertilizer than other plants, such as vegetables. Therefore, it is important to research the fertilization requirements of each plant in your vertical garden to ensure that you are providing them with the right nutrients.

Pests and Diseases

Controlling pests and diseases in a vertical garden is a critical aspect of maintaining healthy plants. Pests and diseases can quickly spread throughout the garden, causing damage to the plants and ultimately affecting their growth and productivity. Here are some tips for controlling pests and diseases in a vertical garden:

Regular inspections: Regular inspections of the plants in your vertical garden are critical to detect any signs of pests or diseases. Look for any damage to leaves, stem, or roots, as well as any unusual spots, discolorations, or growths. Check for pests such as aphids, spider mites, and whiteflies, which are common in many gardens. Inspect for diseases such as powdery mildew, blight, and rust.

Plant selection: One of the easiest ways to prevent pest and disease problems is to select plants that are naturally resistant to pests and diseases. Choose plants that are well-suited for your environment and that are resistant to common pests and diseases in your area. Some examples of plants that are naturally resistant to pests and diseases include herbs like basil, mint, and oregano, and vegetables like tomatoes, peppers, and eggplant.

Proper watering: Proper watering is essential to keep the plants in your vertical garden healthy and resistant to pests and diseases. Overwatering can cause root rot and make the plants more susceptible to disease, while underwatering can stress the plants and make them more vulnerable to pests. It is important to water your plants correctly by providing the right amount of water at the right time.

Organic pest and disease control: Organic pest and disease control methods are a great way to manage pests and diseases in your vertical garden without the use of harmful chemicals. Some examples of organic pest and disease control methods include using beneficial insects, such as ladybugs and lacewings, to control pests, and applying organic pesticides made from natural ingredients like neem oil and pyrethrin.

Chemical pest and disease control: In some cases, chemical pest and disease control may be necessary to manage pests and diseases in your vertical garden. However, it is important to use these products carefully, as they can be harmful to the environment and may also harm beneficial insects and other non-target organisms. Always read and follow the instructions on the product label carefully and use these products only as directed.

Pests can quickly spread throughout the garden, causing damage to the plants and ultimately affecting their growth and yield. Here are some important steps to take to control pests in a vertical garden:

Regular inspections: Regular inspections of the plants in your vertical garden are critical to detect any signs of pests. Inspect your plants regularly for signs of pest activity, including holes in the leaves, damaged or wilted foliage, or tiny insects on the leaves or stems.

Identify pests: The next step in pest control is to identify the pest that is affecting your plants. Some common pests in vertical gardens include aphids, spider mites, whiteflies, and thrips. Different pests require different control methods, so it is important to know which pest you are dealing with.

Natural predators: Natural predators can be an effective way to control pests in a vertical garden. Many beneficial insects like ladybugs, lacewings, and parasitic wasps feed on common pests like aphids and whiteflies, and can be introduced into your garden as a natural control method.

Traps: Pheromone traps and sticky traps can be an effective way to control pests in a vertical garden. Pheromone traps lure male insects into a sticky trap that prevents them from mating, reducing the population of the pest. Sticky traps attract and trap flying insects like whiteflies and thrips, reducing their numbers in the garden.

Organic pesticides: Organic pesticides made from natural ingredients like neem oil, pyrethrin, and spinosad can be an effective way to control pests in a vertical garden. These pesticides work by targeting the nervous system of insects, killing them without harming beneficial insects or other non-target organisms.

Chemical pesticides: In some cases, chemical pesticides may be necessary to control pests in a vertical garden. However, it is important to use these products carefully, as they can be harmful to the environment and may also harm beneficial insects and other non-target organisms. Always read and follow the instructions on the product label carefully and use these products only as directed.

Companion planting: Companion planting is the practice of planting two or more plants together that have a beneficial effect on each other. Some plants, like marigolds, chrysanthemums, and garlic, have natural pest repellent properties and can be planted alongside other plants to help control pests.

Pinching and Pruining
Pinching and pruning are essential techniques for maintaining the shape and size of plants and promoting healthy growth. Here is a detailed guide on how to pinch and prune your plants in a vertical garden:

Pinching: Pinching is a technique used to control the size and shape of plants by removing the growing tips of the plant. This process is done by using your fingers or a sharp pair of scissors to gently pinch off the top leaves and stems of the plant. By removing the growing tip, the plant is forced to branch out and grow fuller and bushier. Pinching is often used for herbs, such as basil, which can grow quite tall if left uncontrolled. It is important to pinch regularly to prevent the plant from flowering, as flowering can reduce the quality and quantity of the harvest.

Pruning: Pruning is the process of removing specific parts of the plant to promote healthy growth and improve its overall shape. Pruning is often used for woody plants, such as tomatoes or fruit trees, but can also be used for many other types of plants. The goal of pruning is to remove dead or damaged branches, improve air circulation and light penetration, and encourage the growth of new shoots and flowers. Pruning can also help control the size of the plant, prevent overcrowding, and encourage the production of high-quality fruit and vegetables.

When pruning, it is important to use sharp, clean tools, such as pruning shears or scissors, to prevent damaging the plant. Start by removing any dead or damaged branches, cutting them back to the nearest healthy growth point. Next, remove any branches that are crossing or rubbing against each other, as this can cause damage to the plant. Finally, prune the plant to the desired shape and size, removing any excess growth to improve air circulation and light penetration.

Tips for Pinching and Pruning:

Pinch and prune regularly to promote healthy growth and prevent overcrowding.

Pinch herbs regularly to prevent flowering and encourage bushier growth.

Prune woody plants to improve air circulation and light penetration and encourage new growth.

Use clean, sharp tools to prevent damage to the plant.

Remove dead or damaged branches immediately to prevent the spread of disease.

Use pruning to control the size of the plant and prevent overcrowding.

Be patient when pruning, taking the time to carefully remove each branch to promote healthy growth.

Harvesting

A well-maintained vertical garden can provide you with a steady supply of fresh herbs, vegetables, and fruits throughout the growing season. Here are some tips for harvesting in a vertical garden:

Harvest at the right time: The timing of your harvest is crucial to ensure the best quality and flavor of your produce. Each plant has its own specific harvesting time, so it's essential to understand the growth cycle of your plants. You can check the growth stages of your plants in the seed packets or by consulting a gardening book or website. For example, some vegetables like tomatoes and peppers are ready to be harvested when they are fully ripe and have a bright color. Others, like leafy greens and herbs, can be harvested when they are young and tender.

Use the right tools: Using the right tools for harvesting can help you avoid damaging your plants and can make your job easier. Some of the tools you might need include garden shears, scissors, or pruning snips for harvesting herbs and vegetables, and a small knife for harvesting fruits.

Harvest frequently: Harvesting frequently can help stimulate the growth of your plants, and it can also help you avoid overripe or rotten produce. Some plants, like herbs, can be harvested multiple times in a season, while others, like tomatoes and peppers, may need to be harvested as soon as they are ripe to avoid overripe produce.

Store your produce properly: Once you've harvested your produce, it's essential to store it properly to ensure it stays fresh for as long as possible. Most vegetables and fruits should be stored in a cool, dry place, while some herbs can be stored in the refrigerator. It's important to avoid washing your produce until you are ready to use it, as excess moisture can cause spoilage.

Compost your scraps: Finally, it's important to compost your vegetable and fruit scraps to help nourish your garden. Composting your scraps can help reduce waste and provide a natural source of fertilizer for your plants. It's easy to compost your scraps by setting up a compost bin or pile in your garden.

Plants for Your Vertical Gardens

Vertical gardens are becoming increasingly popular and are a great way to grow plants in small spaces. When it comes to plants that are suitable for sunny areas, there are several options that can thrive in the sunlight.

One great choice for a vertical garden in a sunny area is tomatoes. They require at least six hours of sunlight per day and prefer well-draining soil. Tomatoes can be grown vertically using trellises, stakes, or cages, which can save space in a small garden. Determinate varieties, which are more compact and require less support, are ideal for vertical gardening.

Peppers are another great choice for a sunny vertical garden. They prefer full sun and well-draining soil, and can be grown using trellises or cages. Hot peppers, such as jalapeños or habaneros, are particularly suited to sunny areas, and can add a spicy kick to a variety of dishes.

Herbs, such as basil, oregano, and thyme, also do well in sunny areas and can be grown vertically. These herbs prefer well-draining soil and full sun, and can add flavor to a variety of dishes. Basil, in particular, is a versatile herb that can be used in salads, soups, and sauces.

Herbs

Herbs are a popular choice for vertical gardening due to their compact size, versatility, and fresh flavors. Many herbs are well-suited for growing in small spaces and can thrive in vertical gardens. Here are some popular herbs that are ideal for vertical gardening:

Basil: Basil is a popular herb that is easy to grow and can add a fresh flavor to many dishes. Basil plants grow quickly, making them an excellent choice for vertical gardens. They are also very attractive, with green leaves that add a pop of color to your garden.

Mint: Mint is a versatile herb that can be used in many dishes and beverages, as well as for medicinal purposes. It is easy to grow and can be very productive in a vertical garden. There are many varieties of mint, each with its unique flavor and scent.

Oregano: Oregano is a perennial herb that is often used in Mediterranean and Italian dishes. It is easy to grow and can be harvested throughout the growing season. Oregano plants can grow up to two feet tall, making them a great choice for a vertical garden.

Thyme: Thyme is another popular herb that is easy to grow and adds a fresh, earthy flavor to many dishes. It is a hardy plant that can thrive in a vertical garden, and its delicate flowers make it an attractive addition to your garden.

Sage: Sage is a perennial herb that is often used in Mediterranean and Italian cuisine. It is easy to grow and can be very productive in a vertical garden. Sage plants can grow up to two feet tall and have a distinctive flavor that adds a unique twist to many dishes.

Rosemary: Rosemary is a hardy perennial herb that is often used in Mediterranean and Middle Eastern cuisine. It is easy to grow and can be harvested throughout the growing season. Rosemary plants can grow up to four feet tall, making them an excellent choice for a vertical garden.

Parsley: Parsley is a popular herb that is often used as a garnish in many dishes. It is easy to grow and can be very productive in a vertical garden. Parsley plants can grow up to two feet tall and have bright green leaves that add a pop of color to your garden.

Lemon balm: Lemon balm is a fragrant herb that can be used for tea, seasoning, and other culinary purposes. It prefers well-draining soil and partial shade. Lemon balm can be grown in containers or in a vertical hydroponic system. It is a great source of antioxidants and can help reduce stress and anxiety.

Chives: Chives are a versatile herb that can be used in a variety of dishes, including soups, salads, and omelets. They prefer well-draining soil and full sun. Chives can be grown in containers, hanging baskets, or in a vertical hydroponic system. They are a great source of Vitamin C and other nutrients.

Bay laurel: Bay laurel is an aromatic herb that is commonly used for seasoning meats, soups, and stews. It prefers well-draining soil and full sun. Bay laurel can be grown in containers, hanging baskets, or in a vertical hydroponic system. It is a great source of antioxidants and can help improve digestion.

Cilantro: Cilantro is a popular herb that is used in Mexican, Thai, and Indian cuisine. It prefers well-draining soil and partial shade. Cilantro can be grown in containers, hanging baskets, or in a vertical hydroponic system. It is a great source of antioxidants and can help reduce inflammation.

Thyme: Thyme is a fragrant herb that is commonly used for seasoning meats, vegetables, and soups. It prefers well-draining soil and full sun. Thyme can be grown in containers, hanging baskets, or in a vertical hydroponic system. It is a great source of Vitamin C and other nutrients.

Sage: Sage is a fragrant herb that can be used for seasoning meats, vegetables, and other dishes. It prefers well-draining soil and full sun. Sage can be grown in containers, hanging baskets, or in a vertical hydroponic system. It is a great source of antioxidants and can help improve cognitive function.

Vegetables

Tomatoes: Tomatoes are one of the most popular vegetables to grow in a vertical garden. They are easy to grow, and there are many varieties available, including cherry tomatoes and beefsteak tomatoes. You can grow them in a trellis, stake, or cage system, and they will provide you with a steady supply of delicious fruits throughout the growing season.

Peppers: Peppers are another popular vegetable to grow in a vertical garden. They come in a range of colors, shapes, and sizes, and they are easy to grow in containers or hanging baskets. You can also grow them on a trellis or stake system, and they will produce a bountiful harvest of spicy or sweet fruits.

Cucumbers: Cucumbers are great vegetables to grow in a vertical garden, as they are vining plants that can be trained to grow up a trellis or stake. They are easy to grow and produce a high yield of refreshing and crisp fruits throughout the growing season.

Salad greens: Salad greens like lettuce, arugula, and spinach are ideal for growing in a vertical garden, as they are fast-growing and do not require a lot of space. You can grow them in containers, hanging baskets, or vertical hydroponic systems, and they will provide you with a constant supply of fresh, healthy greens.

Squash: Squash are vining plants that can be grown on a trellis or stake system, making them an ideal vegetable for vertical gardening. They come in many varieties, including zucchini, yellow squash, and spaghetti squash, and they will produce a bountiful harvest of nutritious and delicious fruits.

Eggplant: Eggplant is a great vegetable to grow in a vertical garden, as it is easy to grow and produces a high yield of fruits. It can be grown in a container or a vertical hydroponic system, and it will provide you with a steady supply of delicious and versatile fruits.

Radish: Radish is a root vegetable that is easy to grow and can be harvested in just a few weeks. It is a cool-season crop that prefers well-draining soil and partial shade. Radish can be grown in containers or in a vertical hydroponic system. They are a great source of Vitamin C and provide a refreshing crunch to salads and sandwiches.

Carrots: Carrots are root vegetables that can also be grown in a vertical garden. They require well-draining soil, and like radish, they prefer partial shade. You can grow carrots in containers or in a vertical hydroponic system. They are a great source of Vitamin A and provide a sweet and crunchy addition to meals.

Garlic: Garlic is a bulb vegetable that can also be grown in a vertical garden. It is easy to grow, and like other bulb vegetables, it prefers well-draining soil. Garlic can be grown in containers or in a vertical hydroponic system. It is a great source of antioxidants and adds a savory flavor to many dishes.

Broccoli: Broccoli is a cool-season crop that can be grown in a vertical garden. It prefers well-draining soil and partial shade. Broccoli can be grown in containers or in a vertical hydroponic system. It is a great source of Vitamin C, fiber, and other nutrients, and is a versatile vegetable that can be used in a variety of dishes.

Spinach: Spinach is a leafy green vegetable that is easy to grow and packed with nutrients. It prefers well-draining soil and partial shade, making it a great choice for a vertical garden. You can grow spinach in containers, hanging baskets, or in a vertical hydroponic system. It is a great source of iron, calcium, and other nutrients, and is a versatile vegetable that can be used in salads, smoothies, and many other dishes.

Fruits

Strawberries: Strawberries are a popular choice for vertical gardens due to their compact size and delicious flavor. They can be grown in containers, hanging baskets, or in a vertical hydroponic system. Strawberries prefer well-draining soil and full sun. They are a great source of Vitamin C and antioxidants.

Blueberries: Blueberries are a delicious and healthy fruit that can be grown in a vertical garden. They prefer well-draining soil and partial shade. Blueberries can be grown in containers or in a vertical hydroponic system. They are a great source of antioxidants and other nutrients.

Raspberries: Raspberries are another fruit that can be grown in a vertical garden. They prefer well-draining soil and partial shade. Raspberries can be grown in containers, hanging baskets, or in a vertical hydroponic system. They are a great source of Vitamin C and fiber.

Grapes: Grapes are a great fruit to grow in a vertical garden, as they can be trained to grow up a trellis or wall. They require well-draining soil and full sun. Grapes can be grown in containers or in a vertical hydroponic system. They are a great source of antioxidants and can be used to make juice, jams, and other tasty treats.

Melons are also a great option for a vertical garden in a sunny area. They require full sun and warm temperatures, making them perfect for outdoor vertical gardens. Melons can be trained to grow vertically using trellises or cages, which can save space in a small garden. Before planting melons in a vertical garden, it's important to choose a variety that is well-suited to your growing conditions. Some varieties of melons, such as cantaloupes and honeydews, do well in warm, dry climates, while others, such as watermelons, require more water and cooler temperatures.

In addition to providing a sweet and refreshing treat, melons can also add an attractive and unique look to a vertical garden. Their sprawling vines and large leaves can provide a lush, tropical feel, and their bright fruits can add a pop of color to any space. With the right care and attention, melons can thrive in a vertical garden and provide a delicious and visually appealing harvest.

Chayote, also known as the vegetable pear, is a tropical plant that is ideal for vertical gardening. It prefers full sun and warm temperatures, and can be grown using trellises or cages. Chayote produces pear-shaped fruits that can be used in a variety of dishes, including stews and salads.

Kiwi is a fruit that is typically grown on a vine, making it a perfect candidate for vertical gardening. Kiwi plants require full sun and well-draining soil, and can be trained to grow on a trellis or other vertical structure. Kiwi plants are also visually appealing, with large, heart-shaped leaves and bright green fruits.

Passion fruit is another tropical plant that is well-suited to vertical gardening in a sunny area. It requires full sun and well-draining soil, and can be grown using a trellis or other vertical structure. Passion fruit produces a tart, flavorful fruit that is commonly used in desserts and beverages.

Legumes

Legumes are another group of plants that are well-suited to a vertical garden in a sunny area. This includes plants such as pease, beans, lentils, and chickpeas. These plants have a vining growth habit, which makes them ideal for growing on a trellis or other vertical structure.

When growing legumes in a vertical garden, it's important to choose a variety that is well-suited to your growing conditions. Some varieties, such as pole beans and climbing peas, are specifically bred for vertical gardening and have a strong vining habit that can grow up to six feet or more. Other varieties, such as bush beans and lentils, have a more compact growth habit and may be better suited to smaller vertical gardens.

Peas are a great option for a vertical garden in a sunny area. They require full sun and well-draining soil, and can be grown using a trellis or other vertical structure. Pea plants are known for their sweet, tender pods, which can be used in a variety of dishes, including salads, stir-fries, and soups.

When growing peas in a vertical garden, it's important to choose a variety that is well-suited to vertical growing conditions. Some varieties, such as snow peas and sugar snap peas, are ideal for vertical gardening because they produce small, tender pods that don't require shelling. These varieties are also known for their strong, vining growth habit, which makes them easy to train on a trellis or other vertical structure.

Pole beans are a type of legume that are specifically bred for vertical gardening. They have a vining growth habit and can grow up to six feet or more, making them ideal for growing on a trellis or other vertical structure. Pole beans are also known for their high yield and delicious flavor, making them a popular choice for many gardeners.

When growing pole beans in a vertical garden, it's important to provide them with a sturdy support structure, such as a trellis, stake, or pole. This will help the plants climb and prevent them from becoming tangled or damaged. Pole beans also require full sun and well-draining soil, and should be watered regularly to prevent the soil from drying out.

One of the advantages of growing pole beans in a vertical garden is that they can be easily harvested without bending or stooping. This can make the harvesting process much easier and more comfortable, especially for gardeners with limited mobility.

Chickpeas, also known as garbanzo beans, are another type of legume that can be grown in a vertical garden in a sunny area. Like other legumes, chickpeas have a vining growth habit and can climb up a trellis or other vertical structure.

Chickpeas are a good source of protein, fiber, and essential vitamins and minerals, making them a healthy addition to your diet. They are also a versatile ingredient that can be used in a wide range of dishes, from salads to soups to hummus.

When growing chickpeas in a vertical garden, it's important to provide them with well-draining soil and regular water. Chickpeas do well in warm, dry climates, so a sunny area is ideal for growing them. Like other legumes, chickpeas also have the ability to fix nitrogen in the soil, which makes them a good companion plant for other plants in your garden.

Chickpeas are typically planted in the spring and require a growing season of about 90-100 days. They can be harvested when the pods turn brown and begin to dry out. After harvesting, the chickpeas can be dried and stored for later use.

Lentils are another type of legume that can be grown in a vertical garden in a sunny area. They are known for their small, disk-shaped seeds that come in a variety of colors, including green, brown, and red.

Lentils are a good source of protein, fiber, and essential vitamins and minerals, making them a healthy addition to your diet. They are also versatile and can be used in a variety of dishes, from soups to salads to stews.

When growing lentils in a vertical garden, it's important to provide them with well-draining soil and regular water. Lentils do well in warm, dry climates, so a sunny area is ideal for growing them. Like other legumes, lentils also have the ability to fix nitrogen in the soil, which makes them a good companion plant for other plants in your garden.

Lentils are typically planted in the early spring and require a growing season of about 90-110 days. They can be harvested when the pods begin to dry out and the seeds inside have hardened. After harvesting, the lentils can be dried and stored for later use.

Hydoponics and Aeroponics Garden Method

Aeroponics and hydroponics are two popular methods for growing plants in a vertical garden. While both methods use a soil-free approach and provide plants with water and nutrients through a solution, there are some key differences between the two:

Root support: In hydroponics, plants are grown in a medium such as perlite, gravel, or coconut coir, which provides support for the roots. In contrast, aeroponics involves suspending the plants in air and misting the roots with a nutrient solution. This allows for maximum exposure to oxygen, which is important for healthy root growth.

Water delivery: In hydroponics, plants are watered from the bottom up using a nutrient solution that is recirculated. This allows the plants to take up water and nutrients as needed. In aeroponics, a fine mist of nutrient solution is sprayed onto the roots. This method allows for more precise control over the amount of water and nutrients delivered to the plants.

Maintenance: Hydroponic systems require regular maintenance, including checking and adjusting pH levels and replacing the nutrient solution. In contrast, aeroponic systems require less maintenance as they are designed to recycle water and nutrients, and only require occasional cleaning.

Cost: Aeroponic systems tend to be more expensive than hydroponic systems, as they require more specialized equipment and technology.

Hydroponics is a method of growing plants in a vertical garden that does not use soil. Instead, plants are grown in a nutrient-rich solution that is delivered directly to the plant roots through a system of tubes or pipes. Hydroponics can be a great option for a vertical garden because it allows for more efficient use of space and water, and can result in higher yields.

To set up a hydroponic vertical garden, you will need a few key components. First, you will need a container or system for holding the nutrient solution. This can be a simple bucket or a more complex system with multiple chambers and pumps. You will also need a growing medium to support the plants, such as coconut coir, perlite, or rockwool. Additionally, you will need a system for delivering the nutrient solution to the plants, such as a drip irrigation system or an ebb and flow system.

To begin, you will need to mix the nutrient solution according to the needs of the plants you will be growing. This will typically involve a combination of macronutrients like nitrogen, phosphorus, and potassium, as well as micronutrients like iron and calcium. Once the nutrient solution is mixed, you can add it to the container or system you will be using.

Next, you will need to add the growing medium to the system and plant your seeds or seedlings. As the plants grow, the nutrient solution will be delivered directly to the roots, which can result in faster growth and higher yields than traditional soil-based growing methods.

One of the key advantages of a hydroponic vertical garden is that it allows you to grow a wide range of plants in a small amount of space. Additionally, because the nutrient solution is delivered directly to the plants, you can reduce water usage and nutrient waste compared to traditional soil-based growing methods. However, hydroponic systems can be more complex and require more maintenance than traditional soil-based gardens, so it's important to do your research and choose a system that will work best for your needs.

Hydroponics is a method of growing plants in a vertical garden without soil, using a nutrient-rich water solution. There are several types of hydroponic systems that are suitable for vertical gardening:

Deep Water Culture (DWC) system: In this system, plants are grown in a container filled with nutrient-rich water, and an air pump provides oxygen to the roots. This system is simple and easy to set up, and is ideal for growing small to medium-sized plants.

Drip irrigation system: In a drip irrigation system, a nutrient-rich water solution is delivered to the plants through a series of tubes and drippers. This system is easy to set up and is ideal for growing plants that require a lot of water, such as tomatoes and cucumbers.

Nutrient Film Technique (NFT) system: In an NFT system, plants are grown in channels that are filled with a thin film of nutrient-rich water. The roots of the plants are exposed to the air, and the nutrient solution flows continuously through the channels. This system is ideal for growing small to medium-sized plants, and is relatively low-maintenance.

Aeroponics system: In an aeroponics system, plants are grown in a container that is suspended in the air, and their roots are misted with a nutrient-rich water solution. This system is ideal for growing plants that require a lot of oxygen, and can lead to faster growth and larger yields.

Ebb and Flow system: In an ebb and flow system, plants are grown in a container that is flooded with a nutrient-rich water solution at regular intervals, and then drained. This system is ideal for growing medium-sized plants, and is relatively low-maintenance.

A wicking system is a hydroponic system that is often used in vertical gardens, as it is a low-maintenance and water-efficient method of growing plants. In a wicking system, plants are grown in containers that sit on top of a water reservoir. A wick made of a material like cotton or felt extends from the bottom of the container into the water, drawing up the nutrient solution to the roots of the plant.

Wicking systems are ideal for small to medium-sized plants, and are relatively low-maintenance, as they do not require a pump or electricity. They are also water-efficient, as the nutrient solution is drawn up to the roots by the wick, so there is no need for excess water or runoff.

However, wicking systems are not suitable for all types of plants, and may not provide enough oxygen to the roots for larger plants or those that require a lot of water. In addition, the wick can become clogged or stop working over time, so it is important to monitor the system and replace the wick if necessary.

Proper drainage is crucial in any hydroponic system, including a vertical garden, as it helps to prevent overwatering and nutrient buildup. Without adequate drainage, excess water can accumulate in the root zone of the plants, leading to root rot and other issues. In addition, standing water can cause nutrient buildup, which can negatively affect the health of the plants.

One way to ensure proper drainage in a vertical garden is to use a growing medium that allows for good drainage. Popular growing mediums for vertical gardens include perlite, vermiculite, coconut coir, and expanded clay pellets. These materials are lightweight and porous, allowing water to drain through quickly and efficiently.

Another key component of proper drainage in a vertical garden is the use of a tray or reservoir to catch excess water. This tray or reservoir should be positioned at the bottom of the garden, and should be deep enough to collect excess water without flooding the plants. A drainage hole or outlet should also be included in the tray or reservoir to allow excess water to drain away.

In some cases, flooding can occur in a hydroponic system if the nutrient solution is not properly mixed or the water level is too high. Flooding can lead to root damage and nutrient buildup, and can ultimately harm the health of the plants. To prevent flooding, it is important to monitor the water level in the reservoir or tray, and to ensure that the nutrient solution is properly mixed and balanced.

Proper drainage is essential for the health of plants in a vertical garden, and should be carefully considered when setting up a hydroponic system. By using a suitable growing medium and ensuring adequate drainage and a properly mixed nutrient solution, a vertical garden can provide a healthy and sustainable environment for plants to thrive.

The aeroponic method is a technique for growing plants in a vertical garden without soil. Instead, plants are suspended in the air and their roots are sprayed with a nutrient-rich mist or water. This method allows plants to grow faster and use less water than traditional soil-based growing methods.

In an aeroponic vertical garden, plants are typically grown in a tower or column structure that is designed to hold the plants and the nutrient solution. The roots of the plants are exposed to the air and sprayed with a nutrient-rich mist or water at regular intervals.

One of the key benefits of the aeroponic method is that it allows plants to grow in a more oxygen-rich environment than traditional soil-based growing methods. This can lead to faster growth, increased nutrient uptake, and stronger, healthier plants.

Another advantage of the aeroponic method is that it allows for more efficient use of water. Since the plants are grown in a mist or water solution, they require much less water than they would in a traditional soil-based garden.

However, it's important to note that the aeroponic method requires more specialized equipment and maintenance than traditional soil-based growing methods. It's also important to ensure that the nutrient solution is properly balanced and that the plants are receiving enough light to grow and thrive.

Water falling, also known as a cascading or waterfall system, is a method of delivering nutrient-rich water to plants in a vertical garden. In a cascading system, water is pumped from a reservoir to the top of the vertical garden, and then flows down through a series of channels or tubes, delivering water and nutrients to the plants as it goes.

One of the benefits of a cascading system is that it provides constant water and nutrient delivery to the plants, which can help to prevent issues like over- or under-watering. The constant flow of water also provides good aeration to the roots, promoting healthy growth and development. In addition, a cascading system can be visually appealing, adding a calming and soothing element to the garden.

However, a cascading system can be more complex and expensive to set up than other hydroponic systems, as it requires a pump and tubing to deliver water and nutrients to the plants. It can also be more difficult to maintain and clean, as the channels or tubes can become clogged with debris or algae over time.

If you want to create a vertical garden that only uses water, you can consider using an aeroponic system. Aeroponics is a hydroponic technique that uses a mist of nutrient-rich water to deliver nutrients to the roots of plants. This method can be highly effective and efficient, as it delivers nutrients and oxygen directly to the roots, promoting fast growth and healthy development.

In an aeroponic system, plants are suspended in a vertical tower, with their roots exposed to the air. A nutrient-rich water solution is then misted onto the roots using a high-pressure pump and specialized nozzles. The mist of water provides both water and nutrients to the roots, and the oxygen-rich environment promotes healthy growth.

One of the main benefits of an aeroponic system is that it uses less water than traditional hydroponic systems, as the misting technique allows for highly targeted delivery of water and nutrients. This can make it a great choice for water-conscious gardeners or those looking to reduce their water usage.

However, aeroponic systems can be more complex and expensive to set up than other hydroponic systems, as they require specialized equipment and maintenance. In addition, they can be more sensitive to changes in the environment or nutrient levels, requiring careful monitoring and adjustment.